better together*

*This book is best read together, grownup and kid.

a akidsco.com

a kids
book
about

a kids book about

GAY PARENTS

by Jonathan & Thomas West

A Kids Co.
Editor Emma Wolf
Designer Rick DeLucco
Creative Director Rick DeLucco
Studio Manager Kenya Feldes
Sales Director Melanie Wilkins
Head of Books Jennifer Goldstein
CEO and Founder Jelani Memory

DK
Delhi Technical Team Bimlesh Tiwary Pushpak Tyagi, Rakesh Kumar
Senior Production Editor Jennifer Murray
Senior Production Controller Louise Minihane
Senior Acquisitions Editor Katy Flint
Acquisitions Project Editor Sara Forster
Managing Art Editor Vicky Short
Managing Director, Licensing Mark Searle

First American edition, 2025
Published in the United States by DK Publishing, 1745 Broadway, 20th Floor,
New York, NY 10019

First published in Great Britain in 2025 by
Dorling Kindersley Limited, 20 Vauxhall Bridge Road, London SW1V 2SA
A Penguin Random House Company

The authorised representative in the EEA is
Dorling Kindersley Verlag GmbH. Arnulfstr. 124, 80636 Munich, Germany

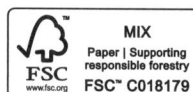

A catalog record for this book is available from the Library of Congress.
A CIP catalogue record for this book is available from the British Library.
ISBN: 978-0-2417-4360-7

DK books are available at special discounts when purchased in bulk for sales
promotions, premiums, fund-raising, or education use. For details, contact:
DK Publishing Special Markets, 1745 Broadway, 20th Floor, New York, NY 10019
SpecialSales@dk.com

Printed and bound in China
www.dk.com
akidsco.com

MIX
Paper | Supporting
responsible forestry
FSC™ C018179

This book was made with Forest
Stewardship Council™ certified
paper – one small step in DK's
commitment to a sustainable future.
Learn more at www.dk.com/uk/
information/sustainability

For Grace, Charlotte, Eleanor, and Henry.

You are loved, you are wanted,
and you will always belong.

Intro
for grownups

How many gay parents do you know? Probably not many, but that's OK. That's why we wrote this book!

Most of us already know that families can look different, but how often do we think about the different types of parents in our communities? We're 2 dads with 4 kids and want to help you teach the kids in your life that there's no right or wrong way to be a family.

We hope that sharing our family's story will help build greater compassion and understanding for gay parents and their kids. Our story shows others they are not alone and can be proud of who they are.

This book is designed to help people learn that the kids of gay parents are loved, wanted, and they belong, and to teach them that families are built on love, no matter who their parents are.

This book is about

FAMI

ILIES.

In our family, there are 2 dads.

Our kids call us

DADDY and **PAPA**.

We even have hats we like
to wear that say that!

Other grownups call us
Jonathan and Thomas.

When we met a very very long time ago, we knew we loved each other.

But, it wasn't until we saw our friends starting families that we knew being a family was what we wanted.

We knew creating a family
was important, amazing, and
the right path forward for us.

So right away, we began.

Together, we started calling people to learn more about adoption.

And we did
LOTS and **LOTS**
of homework.

Although we built our family through adoption, we've found there are many ways to build a family:

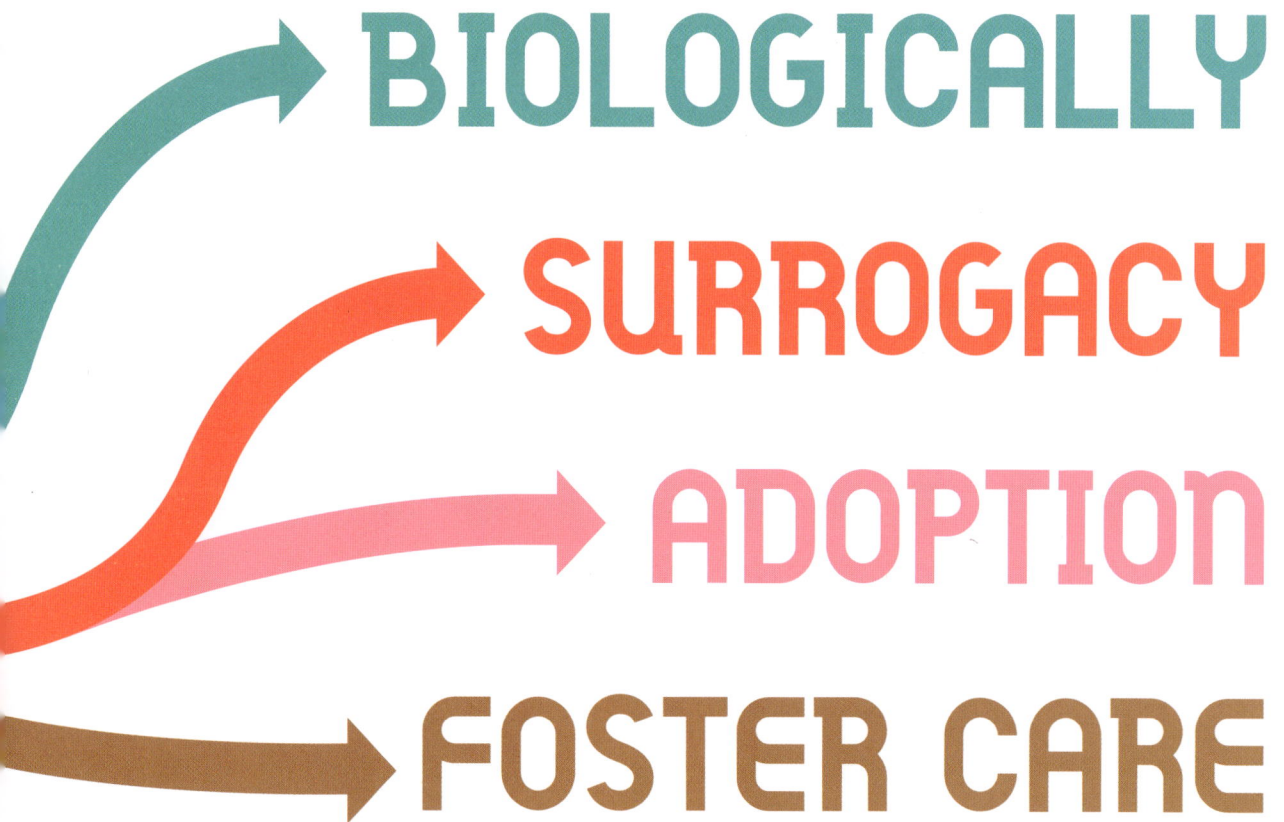

BIOLOGICALLY

SURROGACY

ADOPTION

FOSTER CARE

(to name a few!)

One of our kids tells her friends
that she has a daddy, a papa,
and a birth family.

And another of our kids likes to talk about their first biological family and their second adoptive family.

In our family, it's important that our kids know where they came from.

We build traditions together, and we also work to stay true to our kids' inherited traditions from their birth families.

No matter who we are as a family today, we want our kids to hold on to their own heritage.

When we were growing up, we didn't see people in our communities, on television, or in movies or books who looked like us.

Even though we're grownups now, we didn't know it was possible to have a family, because we hadn't seen one like ours.

Something important to us
is being as visible as we can
to show ourselves, our family,
and EVERYONE that a family
like ours is amazing and possible.

It's something we call...

"ACCEPTANCE THROUGH VISIBILITY."

If we can make a difference
for 1 other person or 1 other family,
we know we've done the right
thing by sharing our story.

And no matter who
you grow up to be, you
can build a family too.

Families look different,
no matter if you have...

A MOM AND A DAD, 2 MOMS,
2 DADS, 1 MOM, 1 DAD,
A GRANDPARENT RAISING YOU,
DIFFERENT SKIN COLORS,
DIFFERENT HAIR TYPES,
OR DIFFERENT TRADITIONS!

Some people think families should only be a mom, a dad, and kids, but we know that's not true.

There are **so** many types of families!

Ours is just 1 kind.

We want you to know,

WHATEVER YOUR FAMILY IS, IT IS EXACTLY RIGHT AND NOT BETTER OR WORSE THAN ANY OTHER FAMILY.

Right now, our family is 2 dads, 4 kids, 3 dogs, 4 ducks, and 5 chickens.

And people always ask if we plan to grow our family.

Our answer is...

WE DON'T KNOW.

Daddy always says no,
but Papa says maybe.

Our answer together
is we'll know when it's right,
just like we always have.

It took a lot of hard work
to build our family.

There were times we weren't
sure it was going to happen.

And we want you to know that the kids of gay parents are wanted, loved, and they belong.

In our house, we like to

BE ADVENTUROUS, SILLY, MOVIES, EAT POPCORN, HA PLAY ON THE SWINGS, RIDE WITH REAL MAPLE SYRUP, READ BOOKS, WEAR LOTS (BECAUSE WE LIVE IN VER

AND ACCEPTING, WATCH
VE BREAKFAST FOR DINNER,
OUR BIKES, EAT PANCAKES
MAKE MOLASSES COOKIES,
OF PLAID AND SWEATERS
MONT), AND BE NORMAL,

just like your family.*

*In our family, whenever anyone toots (farts!), we say, "Ta-da!"

As 2 dads, we do all the things every other parent does.

We change poopy diapers,

make breakfast and school lunches every morning,

pick out clothes,

brush hair AND teeth,

drop kids off at school,

do lots and lots of laundry,

help with homework,

make dinner,

and eat lots of ice cream together.

All parents have a lifelong responsibility to their kids.

We have chosen them and brought them into our lives.

We made the choice to care for, love, support, and raise our kids for as long as we're alive.

It's a lot like the promises we made to one another, out of love, when we got married.

WE CHOSE

TO BE P

TO DO THIS.
ARENTS.

It isn't always easy,
it isn't always fun, but
our family is what
we've chosen.

For all of the times that are hard, there are many more moments which remind us why we chose to start a family in the first place.

Like watching our kids grow,
or the first time our kid said,

"HI, PAPA."

Love truly makes a family.

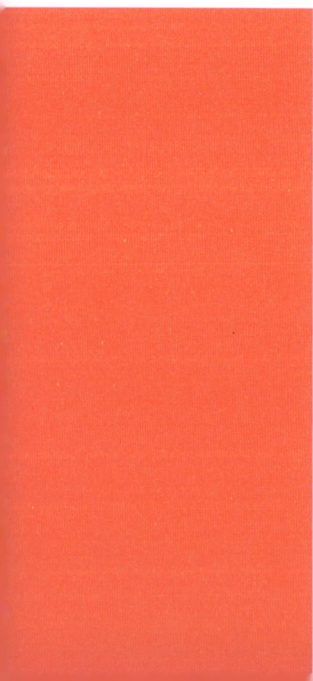

Our family may look different from yours, or maybe we look the same.

But at the end of the day,

LOVE IS WHAT

UNITES US ALL.

Outro
for grownups

Now that you've learned more about gay parents and what diversity looks like, it's time to do the hard part. Talk to your kids about any of the preconceived notions you might have about gay parents and their families. Kids are ready to learn and learn best when the grownups in their lives are honest, transparent, and vulnerable.

To start, read this book again together and be honest about how it made you feel. You can even reach out to us on our socials if you find yourself stuck on something.

Next, share this book with your friends and family. They might have some of the same preconceived notions that you had before reading our book. It's never too early (or late) to start this important conversation.

Finally, help us do the work outside of this book. Share our story whenever the topic comes up. Let's change the ill-conceived narrative that all families look 1 way. All kids deserve a home where they are wanted and loved, and we know it doesn't matter who their parents are to achieve that.

About The Author

Jonathan (he/him) and Thomas (he/him) West wrote this book for their 4 adopted children and the kids of other gay parents.

They believe it is essential for all kids and grownups to know that the makeup of families is different for EVERYONE! And just because someone else's family may look different than yours, it is exactly right, not better or worse.

Jonathan and Thomas believe in sharing their story by being visible to others, so everyone can realize the dream of becoming a parent.

They hope to be the change that allows future parents to be authentic and step into parenthood full of pride and love.

[Instagram] @daddyandpapa   [TikTok] @thedaddyandpapa

[Web] www.daddyandpapa.com   [YouTube] @thedaddyandpapa

Made to empower.

a kids book about **racism**
by Jelani Memory

a kids book about ANXIETY
by Ross Szabo

a kids book about DISABILITY
by Kristine Napper

a kids book about IMAGINATION
by LEVAR BURTON

a kids book about belonging
by Kevin Carroll

a kids book about failure
by Dr. Laymon Hicks

a kids book about GRATITUDE
by Ben Kenyon

a kids book about LIFE ONLINE
by Dave S. Anderson & Blake Fleischacker

a kids book about body image
by Rebecca Alexander

a kids book about IMMIGRATION
by MJ Calderon

a kids book about EMPATHY
by Daron K. Roberts

a kids book about GENDER
by Dale Mueller

a kids book about Love
by ZIGGY MARLEY

a kids book about EQUALITY
by BILLIE JEAN KING

a kids book about MONEY
by Adam Stramwasser

a kids book about FEMINISM
by Emma McIlroy

a kids book about adventure
by Dr. Ben Tertin

a kids book about CLIMATE CHANGE
by Zanagee Artis & Olivia Greenspan

a kids book about CONFIDENCE
by Joy Cho

a kids book about BEING NONBINARY
by Hunter Chinn-Raicht
in partnership with The Gender-Cool Project

Discover more at akidsco.com